T0157984

Simple Truths

—

What You Don't Know Can Destroy You!

Things I Had to Learn to Start Living…

Jacquelyn D. Golden, Ph.D.

WestBow
PRESS
A DIVISION OF THOMAS NELSON

Scripture taken from the King James Version of the Bible.

WestBow Press books may be ordered through booksellers or by contacting:

WestBow Press
A Division of Thomas Nelson
1663 Liberty Drive
Bloomington, IN 47403
www.westbowpress.com
1-(866) 928-1240

Because of the dynamic nature of the Internet, any web addresses or links contained in this book may have changed since publication and may no longer be valid. The views expressed in this work are solely those of the author and do not necessarily reflect the views of the publisher, and the publisher hereby disclaims any responsibility for them.

Any people depicted in stock imagery provided by Thinkstock are models, and such images are being used for illustrative purposes only.

Certain stock imagery © Thinkstock.

ISBN: 978-1-4497-1685-1 (sc)
ISBN: 978-1-4497-1763-6 (e)

Library of Congress Control Number: 2011928747

Printed in the United States of America

WestBow Press rev. date: 6/15/2011

Table of Contents

Foreword by Christopher G. Coleman

This book chronicles Jacquelyn's journey through life as a 'believer' who didn't believe. Yes, it sounds strange, but it's true. She details the importance of studying God's word to avert such dangerous situations. After you read this book you will have an understanding of why listening to others talk about God (including notable leaders) –alone– won't suffice. She also points out simple truths or 'Golden' nuggets that helped her through turbulent times.

Aunt Jackie has left an indelible impression on my personal life. Every time we talk or just hang I am sharpened. She fluently speaks wisdom... oftentimes unaware. I keep pen and paper handy whenever we engage in conversation. I am excited that the world will finally get to read some of the rich words that I have enjoyed since I was a little boy.

Christopher G. Coleman
I Think for You Consulting
Clarksdale, MS

Foreword by Princeola H. Jones

This is a book I wish the entire body of Christ would read. It is about "faith," which we all have to have to be successful in this life. I pray it will give all of us a new outlook on what faith is really about in spite of our choice of churches or denominations. This book has been an eye and heart opener for me, and I hope it will do the same for you. If we allow it, it will bring all of God's people to a new level in Christ Jesus. It will break down the walls that are among many Christian people and the world at large.

My prayer is that this book will help each of us to see and better understand what faith is and that we will apply it to our everyday lives, for faith is divine. And, it comes from God. If we are going to please God, we've got to have it.

My friend, Jackie, keep up the good work! I know where you started years ago. Thanks be unto God for the faith you had in yourself to share these "simple truths" with us today. It's been a long time coming, but it is here now.

Always your friend,
Princeola H. Jones
Syracuse, NY

ACKNOWLEDGEMENTS

This book is dedicated to the memory of my parents, Howard and Christine Golden, who after bringing twelve children (Joe, Earline, Earnestine, LeBertha, Betty, Howard, Jr., Susie, Delores, Al V., Edward Charles, Larry, and Allen) into this world, decided not to abort me even though they were strongly urged to do so. Loving memories of you hold permanent residence in my heart. When asked what you should name me, Joe, the eldest, said, "Too Many!" Thanks for naming me Jacquelyn D. Golden instead. Joe affectionately called me, "Thirteen." And, when he called, I answered.

To my mentor, sister, and friend Dr. Vernice A. Dandridge-Jones, you introduced me to Jesus in a very real way. Thank you! As you are now in the presence of the Lord, your teachings are still with me governing and fashioning my life.

To the various ministries with which I have fellowshipped and labored over the years, thank you for the impartation and for allowing me to help equip individuals for life and ministry.

To my Lord and Savior Jesus Christ, I so give You praise—just because!!!

INTRODUCTION

A significant number of Christians believe the Bible enough to get saved, but they fall short in experiencing the abundant life Jesus said He came to give. As the truth of God's word spreads abroad, Christians will be confronted with a crossroads where each must decide that either this "God of the Bible" is real, and what He says is true, or each must decide that this "God of the Bible" is just another someone to put your hope and trust in, but it would be an exercise in futility to set expectations of Him—expectations that extend beyond saving faith.

Because many ideologies and theories have been instilled deeply in many and in some instances with error but inadvertently so, they have caused many individuals to have misaligned expectations of God, the "Church," and the local church. As a result, many run the risk of becoming disillusioned believers and retarding in their spiritual growth. So, if you are a carrier of the Word of God or plan to become one, make sure you give your hearers the basics so that we minimize the number of God's people who are destroyed because they lack knowledge of some very simple truths.

The intent of this work is to fulfill a promise I made to myself years ago. Because I lacked this knowledge in the early stages of my spiritual growth and development, I made a vow that I would share this collection of basic information with all who would receive it. This collection of information is what rescued me when I was confronted with whether or not I wanted to continue this journey. Instead of bailing out, I decided to throw out a life line. As you grab a hold through reading this text, it is my prayer that it ignites a burning desire in you to want to know more. May the "seek" in you take you to a new place in Him is my prayer.

Chapter 1

Spiritual History 101

More was lost than meets the eye at the point in time when Adam sinned. In fact, many walk from one century into another never recognizing that they have even lost something so precious—the image and power of the true and living God as well as perfect fellowship with Him. The magnitude of that loss was so great that there was no solution that could be given, which was common to man.

Before Adam sinned, the only aspect of God's power that had been revealed was His creative power. After Adam sinned, another aspect of God's power was revealed—His ability to redeem. It is this ability that allows sinful man to gain audience with God and also regain the image of God, which he bore in the beginning before the fall. All who partake of the redemptive work of Jesus Christ at Calvary become members in the family of God commonly referred to as the "Church."

What Is the Church?

The Greek term for the English term "church" is "ekklesia." It is of a compound nature; "ek" means "out," and "kaleo" means "to call" or "to summon." Its literal connotation is "to call out." Who does the calling out? God does it, for Scripture declares that "no man can come to me except the Father which hath sent Jesus draw him . . . ," (John 6:44). So, when a believer says, "I found the Lord and gave my life to Him," the reality is that the Lord called them, and they answered.

The Church is the Body of Christ. And, as the natural body consists of many members so does the Body of Christ. It is a live being, not a still entity. It is a building not made by man and is only observable and detectible by faith through demonstration, signs, wonders, and above all—agape' (the God-kind of love). The Church is the manifested spiritual union of every believer joined together in Christ. The Church is "a community of men who share the divine life that the Church is set apart from every human institution."[1]

We Lost Our Identity—What the Church Is Not

One of the greatest problems that plagues Christendom today is that many assemblies and non-parishioners have misinterpreted the true meaning of the word "church," and as a result have perpetuated the wrong message from generation to generation.

> There are a number of things and groups in existence today called "The Church" but they certainly are not that which the Lord said He would build, nor do they measure up to that which the New Testament means when it speaks of the Church! It is these false concepts of the Church, which have to be rooted out, torn down and plucked up and destroyed before the truth and reality can be built and then replanted.[2]

Scholars report that there are between 115 and 140 occurrences of the term "church" in the New Testament. Kevin Conner, author of the book entitled <u>The Church in the New Testament</u>, believes that those references had nothing to do with a building while others claim that they did. There are several occasions in Scripture that could lead one to believe that the message given by this author is one that uses the term "church" to refer to

2

a location. However, it is understood that the people that are referenced are those that make up the Body of Christ, the Church. So, the message employs duality of meaning. For example, "Unto the church of God which is at Corinth . . . ," (1 Corinthians 1:28) is the introduction of a letter that the Apostle Paul wrote to a group of believers that gathered together consistently. From this passage alone, it is clear that Conner is not hung up on a technicality, but he is trying to convey the importance and a sense of urgency that believers must not over look the real meaning of church.

The most critical Scripture reference to the Church is found in the Book of Matthew chapter 16 and verse 8 where Jesus declared, "Upon this Rock I will build my church; and the gates of hell shall not prevail against it." I along with Conner attempt to urge believers and all mankind to discontinue reducing the meaning of church to that of a material building primarily, for a building made by hand is one that the enemy could easily destroy. The true meaning of Church is that it is a collection of spiritual lively stones, which are joined together by spiritual marrow—Christ, thus forming His body. A more purposeful reference to the location of where the Church comes together for worship might be "assembly" or "gathering." To convey our purpose, the term "church" will be used to refer to the local assembly, and the term "Church" will be used to refer to a relationship to Christ.

Coming to grips with the true meaning of the term "church" in Christendom is critical in that it is the adversary's intent to distract believers by distorting the meaning. It is because of a distorted definition of what the church is that many believers become overwhelmed by the demands of the work of the church. As this concern grows, the concern for the work of ministry diminishes. They lose sight of what is really important to God and replace God's intent with overindulging in what it takes to keep a building and special programming running. They lose their God-focused consciousness.

Denominationalism is another problem that creates chaos in Christendom. The primary root cause for denominationalism is a result of inability to disagree but at the same time remain agreeable—that is the bottom line. It is the crux of the matter! Although denominations are birthed out of very powerful moves of God, many fall prey to concluding that their way is the only way. And, because "we know in part," (1 Corinthians 13:12), no one group can declare that it knows it all.

> Revival normally begins in the glory of God and deteriorates to the glory of Denominations, or a Personality. It goes from the Man to the Movement to the Monument! Having begun in the Spirit, they end up in the flesh. When the Spirit leaves or moves on, then man takes over, forming Doctrinal Statements or Articles of Faith, instituting Creeds, Regulations and Constitutions and By-Laws to try and maintain the Denomination."[3]

The word to Christendom today is to put an end to majoring in the minors. Let's go back to focusing on what Jesus focused on and that which He commanded the disciples and believers to do. That command was and still is:

> Go ye therefore, and teach all nations, baptizing them in the name of the Father, and of the Son, and of the Holy Ghost. Teaching them to observe all things whatsoever I have commanded you: and, lo I am with you always, even unto the end of the world (Matthew 28:18-19).

Who we will become in Him is strongly dependent upon the training and knowledge we receive from those who respond to that great command. That transmission of information should include a clear, concentrated process of making all believers mature disciples. The primary vehicle through which we receive such training occurs through the church or local assembly since many do not grow up with a Christian influence in the household from birth to adulthood. Jesus was able to accomplish this by choosing to neglect a life of luxury and live amongst the twelve. This alone afforded opportunity for the twelve to observe Him close up where they could inquire of Him and get answers instead of having to wait to schedule a meeting with Him.

Most important is that they had an example; they had easy access. Any time individuals spend this magnitude of time together, assuming like character and disciplines are inevitable whether the behaviors observed are natural or spiritual, good or bad. Association brings about assimilation.

You've Got Work to Do

A critical element in understanding the church is discipleship, a process by which individuals are given opportunity to learn and emulate the behavior of those who are not only knowledgeable in the ways of God, but they also practice accordingly—these are they who teach others how to live according to God's standards. The "they" extends far beyond pastors and ministers.

Jesus did not restrict the command to make disciples to pastors only; it is the responsibility of all who partake of His divine love to participate in the making of disciples. It is the pastor's responsibility to ensure that effective processes and systems, which promote the discipleship process, are in place. It is the assignment of the pastor to ensure that the discipleship process is not an assembly-line approach to push as many people through the process in name only. The pastor needs to drive the focal point from being increase in the membership to the focus being on the increase in the number of people who mature in Him. As quiet as it is kept, the reward is linked to our ensuring that those who undergo the new birth experience continue to learn and walk accordingly. We find in John 15:16 the following truth:

> Ye have not chosen me, but I have chosen you, and ordained you, that ye should go and bring forth fruit, and that your fruit should remain: that whatsoever ye shall ask of the Father in my name, he may give it you.

Every believer should be introduced to this process and undergo this process fully understanding that they have been saved to serve. They must understand that they should lead someone else to this same life-giving fountain of life from which they now drink. They should understand that if they partner with your ministry, you are committed to helping them to grow and mature in the knowledge of our Lord, and you will teach them how to disciple someone else. True discipleship as Jesus modeled takes time—it takes time, it takes commitment, it takes genuine love, and it takes relationship. You cannot effectively disciple an individual unless you are willing to pull them in close to you.

So if you are a new believer or if you are a seasoned believer and just happen to stumble across these simple truths, I say to you, "Welcome to the family of God. Learn all you can, and enjoy the new relationship. Understand that it is your responsibility to share this good news with somebody else."

It's Just a Myth—All Bad Things End When One Becomes a Believer

I had a checklist that I inherited upon my accepting Jesus as Lord of my life. And, for the most part I had mastered that list. Somehow, I had the impression that if I satisfied the requirements of that checklist, I would be on God's list of do-gooders. This seemed to have worked for a while; it worked until life began to offer some challenges that fasting, prayer, and quoting scripture did not resolve immediately or as it seemed did not resolve at all. Some matters did not end the way I thought they should have ended—some are still a work in progress. In essence, the outcomes in some situations were not my desired outcomes. How do you explain that? After all, I had satisfied my checklist....

Here's what I learned and continue to learn. The worst thing you can do to invite an individual into the family of God is to say that all of their troubles will end if they accept Jesus as Lord of their life. On the contrary, while this is a great event, it is the moment in time that marks when real trouble begins, for "Many are the afflictions of the righteous: but the Lord delivereth him out of them all," (Psalm 34:17). This is not all bad—there is hope for this situation. And, there is an Answer.

When confronted with challenge, it is important to know up front who is for you and who is against you. Scripture reminds the believer, "Greater is he that is in you than he that is in the world," (1 John 4:4). The lesson that the writer was giving comes to alert the believer that he has some enemies that will rise up and take on different forms. While the enemy takes on various forms, they all have the same goal in mind. And, that is to bring down the redeemed by persuading them to say something other than what God has said and to ultimately disobey Him.

When Jesus stated that He was going to "build a church; and the gates of hell would not prevail against it," (Matthew 16:18), He subtly revealed the enemy of the Church. He more boldly revealed the enemy of the Church in John 10:10 and his strategy, which states, "The thief cometh but for to steal, and to kill, and to destroy: I am come that they might have life, and that they might have it more abundantly." So, the Scriptures admonishes the believer to "be sober, be vigilant; because your adversary the devil, as a roaring lion, walketh about, seeking whom he may devour," (1 Peter 5:8). It is for such reasons that it is important to count up the cost, but unfortunately many believers are converted before any measure of discipleship takes place. They are converted and do not fully understand the price.

Salvation is free but the walk requires a lot from us. Life's journey is not a cake walk just because one is saved. As stated before, it is indeed quite the contrary! The minute one accepts Jesus Christ as Lord and Savior and asks for forgiveness of sin, he becomes a moving target, that which the chief enemy of the Church pursues like a raging bull. Like unbelievers, believers have valley experiences. The difference between a believer's valley experience and an unbeliever's valley experience is that one is in right fellowship with God and the other is not. Because the believer is joint heir with Jesus Christ, he is endowed with benefits that are solely linked to that relationship. The believer can "boldly come to the throne of grace and can obtain mercy and grace to help in time of need," (Hebrews 4:16) in a way that the unbeliever might not even know exists. The unbeliever must solely rely upon the mercies of God until he becomes reunited with the Father through Jesus Christ whereby he can partake of a continuous flow of benefits that only come through a continuous flow of fellowship. Nevertheless, they both go through valley experiences. The operative phrase is "go through." Like the disciples, today's believers must understand that a part of following Christ includes suffering. The challenge is to respond like the disciples when they were commanded by the council to stop teaching in the name of Jesus (Acts 5:12-40). Instead of obeying the council, they chose to obey God's command to go and teach all nations; but in so doing, they were beaten and imprisoned. Once released, "they departed from the presence of the council, rejoicing that they were counted worthy to suffer shame for his name," (Acts 5:41). What a testimony!

The disciples could respond as described above because they understood this truth:

> The weapons of our warfare are not carnal, but mighty through God to the pulling down of strongholds; casting down imaginations, and every high thing that exalteth itself against the knowledge of God, and bringing into captivity every thought to the obedience of Christ (2 Corinthians 10:4-5).

Every believer has an arsenal of weaponry to choose from in times of battle. The solution should be based upon what God has told the believer concerning how to adorn himself in battle and how to fight against things that cannot be seen by the natural eyes. God's arsenal of weaponry is defined in Ephesians chapter 6 verses 10-18.

> Finally my brethren, be strong in the Lord, and in the power of his might. Put on the whole armor of God that ye may be able to stand against the wiles of the devil. For we wrestle not against flesh and blood, but against principalities, against powers, against the rulers

of the darkness of this world, against spiritual wickedness in high places. Wherefore take unto you the whole armour of God that ye may be able to with stand in the evil day, and having done all, to stand. Stand therefore, having your loins girt about with truth, and having on the breastplate of righteousness; And your feet shod with the preparation of the gospel of peace; Above all, taking the shield of faith, wherewith ye shall be able to quench all the fiery darts of the wicked. And take on the helmet of salvation, and the sword of the Spirit, which is the word of God: Praying always with all prayer and supplication in the Spirit, and watching thereunto with all perseverance and supplication for all saints.

This passage is a popular one. It is one that many ministers use as a first-time message. It is often presented with such oratory skill and life, but what does this really mean? Understanding how to put on the armour of God for tenured believers is challenging. And, it is even more challenging for the new convert. Let's examine this passage more closely. When a draftee is called to serve in the United States Armed Forces, he undergoes extensive training in war tactics, strategies, and weaponry. But, before he ever gets involved with the weapons, he is stripped of his own belief system and system of values and assumes loyalty to a code dictated by the government of the United States. Likewise, it is for the believer as he is engrafted into the family of God. The believer is challenged to "be transformed by the renewing of his mind," (Romans 12:2), and he is further challenged to let the mind that was in Christ Jesus be also in him (Philippians 2:5). As the natural mind becomes subject to the General in the person of the Holy Spirit, he begins to put on the armour of God through faith. According to Kevin J. Conner,

The armour of God is an expression that symbolizes the combat equipment of a Christian soldier who fights against spiritual wickedness; the full resources of God, which are available to all who take up the cross and follow Christ. Because our spiritual enemy is stronger than we are,[4] 'we must put on the whole armour of God,' (Ephesians 6:11-13).

It is by faith that the believer puts on both defensive and offensive armour for protection and for conquering. This is a truth that has to be more loudly proclaimed because there are so many waging in a war, but they do not know who they are fighting, and they do not know how to fight against the unseen. And, because they do not know how to fight against the unseen, many Christians are living in isolation of the manifold blessings of God. If you were to go by the examples in the Scriptures, you would find that in the greatest battle ever recorded, Jesus, who is the Word, had to use the Word to fight the temptations of the enemy. The question that Christendom must address is, "If He who was the Word had to use the Word in His own defense, how much more is the believer to do the same?"

Knowing the Word, along with applying the Word is as paramount to the believer as breathing oxygen is to living things. Oxygen can be ever so present, but if one does not employ the mechanics of breathing, he will surely die. We must know the Word and enforce it by faith in times of battle. The Word will destroy the snares of the enemy. Knowing this truth alone can turn on the heat under the seat of the war against spiritual retardation and defeat. And, so one's declaration has to be: In spite of what I feel, see, hear, or think, His word is true and will not return unto me void! It will accomplish what God has commanded it to accomplish.

We Win!!!

What makes a novel or movie interesting is not knowing how it will end. And, as one goes through each chapter or scene, it is fun and challenging to try to predict what the outcome will be. Well, the scenes of life can be likened to a movie. And, I am breaking my personal rule about movies, which is not to reveal the end. It is imperative that I do so in this instance.

The difference between a fictional movie and the scenes of life is that the outcome has already been revealed in the Scriptures. Taking the time to read and begin to understand the truths that lie between Genesis and Revelation, all would discover that in the end, the Church of Jesus Christ wins! This should encourage the new convert and further encourage the tenured saint because this lets all know that living a life separated unto God is indeed worth the living. The fight of life in which believers are engaged is a fixed fight. All believers have to do is adorn themselves with the armour of God, stand, and swing the sword of the Word believing that he will receive all that is needed to overcome the battle. When Jesus, who is the Word, defended Himself against the enemy as he tempted Him in the wilderness, in every phase of the temptation, Jesus used the Word. I say to you again: If the Word who is the Word had to use the Word in His own defense, the same applies to the believer.

The believer must come to grips with the fact that the battle in which he is engaged is between God and the enemy. Thus, the believer must be very alert because they are the ones who get caught in the middle of the crossfire. But, that is fine because "he that dwells in the secret place of the Most High, shall abide under the shadow of the Almighty," (Psalms 91:1). This abiding extends even beyond the grave into everlasting life. There is no greater safety than this.

END NOTES

[1]Lawrence O. Richards, <u>Christian Education: Seeking to Become Like Jesus</u>, (Grand Rapids: Zondervan Publishing House, 1975), 13.

[2]Kevin J. Conner, <u>The Church in the New Testament</u>, (Portland: City Bible Publishing, 1982), 9.

[3]Ibid., 10.

[4]<u>Nelson's Illustrated Bible Dictionary</u>, (Nashville: Thomas Nelson Publishers, 1986), 9.

Chapter 2

Getting Results on This Journey

One day I was saved, and the kick off into the new life was exciting. Life was good for this twelve-year old kid! As time progressed in my journey, what I was being taught and what little I could comprehend did not look like the results the Bible said I would experience. My initial exposure to prayer was presented as some mystical experience in which one is caught up into a state of being where awareness of one's surroundings ceases to exist. So as a youngster, my inclination was not to pray like that, it was to walk in fear of this expression. That expression along with imbalance of theory versus actuality provoked me to anger and ultimate disappointment in many instances. This state of unrest started me to consider why the disciples asked Jesus to teach them how to pray. I believe what they were really asking was that He would teach them how to get the results that He got—this is what I meant when I made the same request.

In order for this to have happened, Jesus had to teach the disciples how to communicate with the Father. In its simplest definition, prayer is a conversation between God and the one praying. This simple definition formed the basis of what I thought prayer entailed. As I grew, I learned that prayer is man talking to God; but, more importantly, it is man's waiting in a posture where God can talk to man. It is in this exchange that man expresses his needs or concerns and at the same time, it is one of the means through which God comforts man and expresses His heart and expectations of man. Prayer is also the means through which believers confess their sins and/or inadequacies before God, and it is also the means through which believers minister to the Lord in praise, thanksgiving, and worship. Prayer is a deliberate choice to set aside time to entertain the presence of God.

I have learned that eloquence of speech and knowing a multitude of words does not make prayer effective. What makes prayer effective is that the one praying knows that this action is a response to his awesome God who is solely responsible for his salvation and is the only One who is able to answer prayer. What makes prayer effective is the condition of the heart. God knows when we are sincere, and He knows when we are simply playing puppet master or simply trying to yank His chain to give us what we want and when we want it. I have learned to verify the contents of my heart by praying the prayer David prayed: "Examine me, O Lord, and prove me; try my reins and my heart," (Proverbs 26:2). Scan my heart and emotions and remove any impurities—take it away.

Once I grasped the simplicity of prayer, abundant living through Christ began to manifest, and much was accomplished as is written in James 5:16b, "The effectual fervent prayer of a righteous man availeth much." Does this mean that I always get what I pray for? No! It means that before I enter into prayer, I go in with the preconceived notion that whatever He speaks to me, I will accept and obey. As I grow, mature, and learn to think like Jesus did, the more my desired outcomes look like His desired outcomes.

Types of Prayer

"The men and women of the Old Testament saw God as their Father and felt that prayerful communion with Him was a natural part of life."[1]

David builds a case for consistence and order in daily prayer. The repetition of the phrase 'in the morning' justified an alternate translation: 'morning by morning.' Also significant is the psalmist's selection of the Hebrew word 'arak' ('direct') in his declaration that he would 'direct' his petitions to God daily.[2]

As you walk through the Scriptures, you will find that there are many types of prayer. It is vitally important that believers understand that there are several different types of prayer. Why is this so important? Let's use the following scenario to shed some light on this thought. When an infant is learning to distinguish between bologna and salami, he will see salami and ask for bologna and vice versa. But, there comes a point in time when the parent will begin to expect the child to reach a level of maturity and come to know the difference between the two. The parents will begin to require specificity. The believer's interactions with God are very similar. As new babes in Christ, prayers seem to take on no specific form. All that the new babe knows is that he means what he says, and he needs God to act on his behalf now. This will go on for so long, but there comes a point where specificity or the lack thereof could make the difference in the life or death of a situation. It is like trying to reach God and He is tuned in on a FM station, but the one praying is tuned in to an AM station. In order to get on the same wavelength, it is important to know the various prayer channels so that one can aim for the spiritual bull's eye and hit that target and not simply land somewhere in the vicinity. The various prayer channels include the following: petitions, confession, agreement, chiding prayers, intercessory prayers, praise and thanksgiving, and faith.

Prayer of Petition

The prayer of petition is one in which one asks God with fervor to meet a dire need. There are many Bible personalities that employed the prayer of petition. Consider Hannah, one of the wives of Elkanah of the Old Testament. Elkanah's other wife was named Peninah. Knowing that the ultimate expression of a woman's love for her husband was to bear him a son, Peninah provoked Hannah by bragging about her ability to please their husband in this manner. She provoked her to the point that Hannah ached with pain; she wept and did not eat for days. This provoking, although deemed negative, was the catalyst that moved Hannah to another level of prayer. Up to this point she was a miserable woman. Now she was a miserable woman bombarding heaven to release resources that only God could give. Hannah prayed with such sincerity that she vowed a vow with the intent to keep it. In this vow she promised God that if He gave her a boy child, she would set him aside for His use. The critical point here is that Hannah was very sincere, and she was very specific. I believe that if she had received a girl child, she would have continued to pray until she received exactly what she had requested. This should encourage the believer not to settle for less than what he has petitioned God for as long as he has prayed according to the will of God.

Prayer of Agreement

The prayer of agreement is almost always associated with Matthew 18:18-20, which states,

> And I will give unto you the keys of the kingdom of heaven: and whatsoever you bind on earth shall be bound in heaven; and whatsoever thou shalt loose on earth, shall be loosed in heaven. Again I say, That if two of you shall agree on earth as touching any thing that they shall ask, it shall be done of my Father which is in heaven. For where two or three are gathered together in my name, there am I in the midst of them.

If that is the case, why do many believers not get their desired results when they bind and loose certain things? Some believe that we must first examine this passage more closely and consider who this passage was written to as well as consider whether or not binding and loosing is a command to believers at large.

If you examine this passage as restated in Matthew 16:13-19, new insight is given. Jesus posed a question to the disciples, saying,

> Whom do men say that I the Son of man am? And they said, some say that thou art John the Baptist; Some, Elias; and others Jeremias, or one of the prophets. He saith unto them, But whom say ye that I am? And Simon Peter answered and said Thou art the Christ, the Son of the living God. And Jesus answered and said unto him, Blessed art thou Simon Barjona: for flesh and blood hath not revealed it unto thee, but my Father which is in heaven. And I say also unto thee, That thou art Peter and upon this rock I will build my church and the gates of hell shall not prevail against it. And I will give unto thee the keys of the kingdom of heaven: and whatsoever you bind on earth shall be bound in heaven; and whatsoever thou shalt loose on earth, shall be loosed in heaven.

So, was this access given to the disciples alone, or is this access given to all who believe? Additional information is given in verse 19: "Again I say unto you, That if two of you shall agree on earth as touching any thing that they shall ask, it shall be done for them of my Father which is in heaven." Notice that verse 19 begins with "again" which means once more or a repeat of something previously said or done. It seems to refer back to verse 18 which outlines the principles concerning binding and loosing of things on the earth and in heaven. Verse 18 is restated in a different way in verse 19, thus they both yield the same results. This is good news for the believer because Jesus makes it clear that He is giving that power to the Church.

Like all other types of prayer mentioned in this study, binding and loosing works commensurate to one's knowledge of, faith in, and obedience to the Word of God. To apply the principle of binding and loosing without all three of these elements can result in believers' setting up expectations of God, expectations to which He never committed. The ultimate adverse outcome will be misaligned expectations. And, the church scene will become worse than what it is as too many are running around touching and agreeing, but nothing ever happens. There is something indeed wrong with this picture.

Prayer of Chiding

Chiding prayers are those that allow the believer to get some things off of his chest by expressing them to God. This type of prayer allows the believer to be honest with himself about how he feels when he is angry with life and man and even when he is angry with God. A perfect example of this is Jonah. See the passages below.

> The word of the LORD came unto Jonah the son of Amittai, saying, Arise, go to Nineveh, that great city, and cry against it; for their wickedness is come up before me, Jonah rose up to flee unto Tarshish from the presence of the LORD, and went down to Joppa; and he found a ship going to Tarshish: so he paid the fare thereof, and went down into it, to go with them unto Tarshish from the presence of the LORD," (Jonah 1:1-6).

Instead of doing exactly as he was commanded, the Scriptures let us know that Jonah boarded a ship, which created havoc for the mariners as a stormed arose tossing them to and fro. This took place until the mariners came to the realization that this trouble began when Jonah boarded the ship. So, they threw him overboard. Jonah was then swallowed by a whale. When Jonah came to his senses regarding his carrying out the will of God, the whale regurgitated him out according to Jonah Chapter 2:1-10:

> Then Jonah prayed unto the LORD his God out of the fish's belly, And said, I cried by reason of mine affliction unto the LORD, and he heard me; out of the belly of hell cried I, and thou heardest my voice. For thou hadst cast me into the deep, in the midst of the seas; and the floods compassed me about: all thy billows and thy waves passed over me. Then I said, I am cast out of thy sight; yet

I will look again toward thy holy temple. The waters compassed me about, even to the soul: the depth closed me round about, the weeds were wrapped about my head. I went down to the bottoms of the mountains; the earth with her bars was about me forever: yet hast thou brought up my life from corruption, O LORD my God.

When my soul fainted within me I remembered the LORD: and my prayer came in unto thee, into thine holy temple. They that observe lying vanities forsake their own mercy. But I will sacrifice unto thee with the voice of thanksgiving; I will pay that that I have vowed. Salvation is of the LORD. And the LORD spake unto the fish, and it vomited out Jonah upon the dry land.

The story continues in Jonah Chapter 3:1-10:

And the word of the LORD came unto Jonah the second time, saying, Arise, go unto Nineveh, that great city, and preach unto it the preaching that I bid thee. So Jonah arose, and went unto Nineveh, according to the word of the LORD. Now Nineveh was an exceeding great city of three days' journey. And Jonah began to enter into the city a day's journey, and he cried, and said, Yet forty days, and Nineveh shall be overthrown. So the people of Nineveh believed God, and proclaimed a fast, and put on sackcloth, from the greatest of them even to the least of them.

For the word came unto the king of Nineveh, and he arose from his throne, and he laid his robe from him, and covered him with sackcloth, and sat in ashes. And he caused it to be proclaimed and published through Nineveh by the decree of the king and his nobles, saying, Let neither man nor beast, herd nor flock, taste any thing: let them not feed, nor drink water: But let man and beast be covered with sackcloth, and cry mightily unto God: yea, let them turn every one from his evil way, and from the violence that is in their hands. Who can tell if God will turn and repent, and turn away from his fierce anger, that we perish not? And God saw their works, that they turned from their evil way; and God repented of the evil, that he had said that he would do unto them; and he did it not.

Jonah 4:1-11 sheds more detail about Jonah's chiding prayer:

But it displeased Jonah exceedingly, and he was very angry. And he prayed unto the LORD, and said, I pray thee, O LORD, was not this my saying, when I was yet in my country? Therefore I fled before unto Tarshish: for I knew that thou art a gracious God, and merciful, slow to anger, and of great kindness, and repentest thee of the evil. Therefore now, O LORD, take, I beseech thee, my life from me; for it is better for me to die than to live.

Then said the LORD, Doest thou well to be angry? So Jonah went out of the city, and sat on the east side of the city, and there made him a booth, and sat under it in the shadow, till he might see what would become of the city. And the LORD God prepared a gourd, and made it to come up over Jonah, that it might be a shadow over his head, to deliver him from his grief. So Jonah was exceeding glad of the gourd. But God prepared a worm when the morning rose the next day, and it smote the gourd that it withered.

And it came to pass, when the sun did arise, that God prepared a vehement east wind; and the sun beat upon the head of Jonah, that he fainted, and wished in himself to die, and said, It is better for me to die than to live. And God said to Jonah, Doest thou well to be angry for the gourd? And he said, I do well to be angry, even unto death.

Then said the LORD, Thou hast had pity on the gourd, for the which thou hast not laboured, neither madest it grow; which came up in a night, and perished in a night: And should not I spare Nineveh, that great city, wherein are more than sixscore thousand persons that cannot discern between their right hand and their left hand; and also much cattle?

And, the dialogue between God and Jonah continues on . . . . In this chapter, it is clearly revealed that God allowed Jonah to express his anger. Also, note that God taught some lessons using somewhat painful techniques. So, chiding prayers position one to freely express his anger, but one must be willing to accept the various techniques God will choose to use in chastening those He loves.

Prayer of Intercession

Intercession, as it is known today in many Pentecostal circles, is misunderstood. Proof that it is misunderstood is that it is treated as a special assignment given to a particular group of people when it is an assignment that is given to every believer. This vein of thought is dangerous if one believes this to be true of intercession, for believing this will lead to an empty or non-existent prayer life. This is a misunderstanding that must be corrected if believers will experience an abundant life in Christ. Romans 8:26-27 states:

> Likewise the Spirit also helpeth our infirmities: for we know not what we should pray for as we ought: but the Spirit itself maketh intercession for us with groanings which cannot be uttered. And he that searcheth the hearts knoweth what is the mind of the Spirit, because he maketh intercession for the saints according to the will of God.

Romans 8:34 states that it is Christ who also maketh intercession for us. In the same manner that the Holy Spirit and Jesus make intercession for us, the same should be our priority for one another. Afterall, "we have the mind of Christ," (1 Corinthians 2:16). Intercession or "huperentugchano" in the

Greek, and as depicted in Romans 8:26 means to apply one's self to intercede for another, or simply put, intercession is a type of prayer where the one who prays, prays for an individual or individuals as if it were his own plight for which he is praying. Paul gives us a list of those who should be added to Timothy's on-going prayer list. And, if this was a part of the believers' responsibility in that day, it is no different today. Paul writes to Timothy,

> I exhort therefore, that, first of all, supplications, prayers, intercessions, and giving of thanks, be made for all men; For kings, and for all that are in authority; that we may lead a quiet and peaceable life in all godliness and honesty (1 Timothy 2:1-2).

Paul goes on to say that "this is good and acceptable in the sight of God our Saviour," (1 Timothy 2:3). Believers intercede for others because it is God's will that "all men be saved, and all will come into the knowledge of truth," (1 Timothy 2:4).

Prayer of Praise / Thanksgiving

Praying the prayer of praise and thanksgiving dates back to the Old Testament. For example, "And Mattaniah the son of Micha, the son of Zabdi, the son of Asaph, was the principal to begin the thanksgiving in prayer: and Bakbukiah the second among his brethren, and Abda the son of Shammua, the son of Galal, the son of Jeduthun," (Nehemiah 17:2). It is the will of God that believers pray the prayer of thanksgiving. He commands the believer to "be careful for nothing; but in every thing by prayer and supplication with thanksgiving let your requests be made known unto God," (Philippians 4:6). When God commands one to pray, it is in his best interest to do just that—pray. When we obey, we receive the associated benefits that are only linked to obedience.

There are many instances of prayer through thanksgiving throughout the Scriptures along with their associated outcomes. This study highlights a few to show the believer that this type of prayer is essential to the believer. In the action that takes place in Jonah Chapter 2 verses 1 and 2, once Jonah humbled himself and sacrificed unto God with the voice of thanksgiving and paid what he had vowed, the LORD spake unto the fish, and it vomited out Jonah upon the dry land.

David employed this type of prayer almost always. In one of his prayers he prayed,

> Judge me, O LORD; for I have walked in mine integrity: I have trusted also in the LORD; therefore I shall not slide. Examine me, O LORD, and prove me; try my reins and my heart. For thy loving kindness is before mine eyes: and I have walked in thy truth. I have not sat with vain persons, neither will I go in with dissemblers. I have hated the congregation of evil doers; and will not sit with the wicked. I will wash mine hands in innocency: so will I compass thine altar, O LORD: That I may publish with the voice of thanksgiving, and tell of all thy wondrous works (Psalms 26:1-7).

David's sole purpose was to be a testimony for the true and living God. So, his requests were made not just so that his personal needs would be met, but so that he could offer up thanksgiving and declare to the people that God was his source.

There is a fine line between giving thanks versus praying the prayer of thanksgiving. Earlier prayer was defined as a conversation between God and man. It is a participatory dialogue between the two. So, when the prayer of thanksgiving is employed, the believer engages God in conversation just to say thank you.

Prayer of Faith

The prayer of faith is the foundation for all other types of prayer.

The most meaningful prayer comes from a heart that places its trust in the God who has acted and spoken in the Jesus of history and the teachings of the Bible. God speaks to us through the Bible, and we in turn speak to Him in trustful, believing prayer.[3]

Because God is Omnipotent, Omniscient, and Omnipresent, we can be sure that He hears us when the prayer of faith serves as the foundation for any prayer. What is the prayer of faith? The prayer of faith is a most potent type in that "the prayer of faith shall save the sick, and the Lord shall raise him up; and if he have committed sins, they shall be forgiven him," (James 5:15). So, the prayer of faith is one that serves a dual purpose. It has the power to both heal the natural and the spiritual in one clean sweep if one has sinned. This power is given to the believer and not just the elders of the church. This is good news. Recall Mark Chapter 11 where Jesus cursed a fig tree because it was not bearing fruit, and the tree died as a result of His command. The disciples were amazed. Jesus told them that they could do the same if they would do one thing:

> Have faith in God . . . whoever says to this mountain be thou cast into the sea and does not doubt in his heart, but shall believe that those things which he saith should come to pass; he shall have whatsoever he saith. Therefore I say unto you, What things so ever ye desire, when ye pray, believe that ye receive them, and ye shall have them (Mark 11:23-24).

Jesus said that if we believe when we pray, we have that for which we have prayed. At that precise moment, it belongs to us. So, with this type of kingdom access, why are so many believers living contrary to what the Scriptures say that they can possess? Part of the problem is that there is little being taught concerning the various types of prayer. And, if faith is to come to serve as foundation for prayer, then hearing the Word is imperative. In order for hearing to take place, someone has to say something. Once believers are positioned in a posture of prayer founded upon unwavering faith, they can rest assured that God hears them and that they will receive what they need.

Now to add balance to all that has been said regarding prayer,

> If we are beginners, we need to put our faith into action in a beginning way and choose subjects for prayer that lie within our

limited faith experience . . . we will still need to recognize our limitations.[4]

As one becomes more fluent in exercising his faith, he will be able to pray for the removal of mountains that are much bigger. The results of prayer will always be commensurate with one's experience in the Word and experience in exercising faith.

Prayer of Confession

As the believer looks into the mirror of the Word, the consciousness of his mind regarding his coming short of the glory of God grows, and the heart becomes more sensitive to sin. When the believer has a true encounter with God, one of two things will always happen: Either he will choose to change or he will deliberately choose to remain the same. As in Isaiah's case, he chose to change and cried out, "Woe is me for I am undone, because I am a man of unclean lips, and I dwell in the midst of a people of unclean lips, for my eyes have seen the King, the Lord of hosts," (Isaiah 6:5). Sin is so devastating because it alienates man from God. This is why it is so important that we live in a repentant posture for God is "faithful and just to forgive us our sins, and to cleanse us from all unrighteousness," (1 John 1:9). That work is finished!

One of the truths I came to grips with after 20 years in my walk in Christ, is that even though I had mastered the rules on my inherited checklist, I was a sinner. While I was not living the wild life, if you will, I was made aware that we can fall short in sin and not be readily aware of it. So, for years I walked around lying to myself that there was no sin in my life and grossly unaware that the Scriptures say, "If we say that we have not sinned, we make him a liar, and his word is not in us," (1 John 1:10). And, so this is why I believe it is important to share this truth. It is so sad to walk around thinking that all is well when the truth of the matter is that all is not well. When the believer fully understands the mercy and grace combination that is applied in our stead, we will extend that mercy and grace to others whether saved or not saved, whether saint or sinner. We will be a channel for the grace to abound and begin to see people as souls that God loves.

The Model Prayer

When the disciples asked Jesus to teach them to pray, Jesus responded with a lesson on prayer that would always result in God-desired results. This prayer is considered by many to be the model prayer. In the Gospel of Matthew, this prayer was a part of Jesus' Sermon on the Mount where he emphasized that "prayer should not be an attempt to get God's attention by repeating words. Instead, it should be a quiet, confident expression of needs to our heavenly Father."[5] Luke's account reveals Jesus' teaching on how to pray and what to pray (Luke 11:2). While it is good to use this model in prayer, believers should not make this a law as they apply this example to their lives and lead others to believe that if they do not pray this prayer verbatim, they are not connecting with God. Jesus said, "When you pray, pray like this—He did not say, "Pray this." The table on the next page gives a general analysis of the model prayer as recorded in Matthew 6:9-13.

TABLE 6

THE MODEL PRAYER

The Lord's Prayer	
"Our Father which art in heaven, Hallowed be they name."	The first part of the prayer concerns the glory of God. We call him "Father," a term which only His children by faith in Christ may rightly use. We request that God's name be "hallowed," or honored as holy. It is the mission of God's people to spread the reputation of His name throughout the world (Ezekiel 36:22-23).

"Thy kingdom come. Thy will be done in earth, as it is in heaven."	This segment of the prayer requests that God's kingdom come. The desire is for His way of doing things in heaven to be done the same way in the earth. This means that we acknowledge God as ruler of the world and obey His will. His will shall be done perfectly when our Lord returns.
"Give us this day our daily bread."	Requests relating to our own needs include food for each day, forgiveness, and help in temptation. Workers in Jesus' time often were hired day by day. They knew their daily need.
"And forgive us our debts, as we forgive our debtors."	Our forgiveness for sin comes only through the death of Christ on the cross. Our experience of that forgiveness requires us not to hold things against others and not to deny God's forgiveness.
"And lead us not into temptation, but deliver us from evil:"	Lead us not into temptation, but deliver us from evil means, "Do not let us be tested so that we fall into sin; save us from the power of the evil one satan."
"For thine is the kingdom, and the power, and the glory, forever. Amen." (Matthew 6:9-13)	The conclusion of the Lord's Prayer attributes all power and glory to God forever, through all eternity. This part of the prayer should be evident in our lives each day as we seek to do God's will on earth as His disciples.

Source: <u>Nelson's Illustrated Bible Dictionary</u>, (Nashville: Thomas Nelson Publishers, 1986), 653. [6]

More Than a Sparrow's Portion

Some of the best news that I have ever heard is found in Matthew 6:31 where in brief, I learned that Jesus is concerned about my needs. He stated,

Therefore take no thought, saying, What shall we eat? Or, What shall we drink? Or, Wherewithal shall we be clothed? For after all these things do the Gentiles seek: for your heavenly Father knoweth that ye have need of all these things. But seek ye first the kingdom of God, and his righteousness; and all these things shall be added unto you. Take therefore no thought for the morrow: for the morrow shall take thought for the things of itself.

The news gets even better in Luke 12:6-7, 22-32:

Are not five sparrows sold for two farthings, and not one of them is forgotten before God? But even the very hairs of your head are all numbered, Fear not therefore: ye are of more value than many sparrows. And he said unto his disciples, Therefore I say unto you, Take no thought for your life, what ye shall eat; neither for the body, what ye shall put on. The life is more than meat, and the body is more than raiment.

Consider the ravens: for they neither sow nor reap; which neither have storehouse nor barn; and God feedeth them: how much more are ye better than the fowls? And which of you with taking thought can add to his stature one cubit? If ye then be not able to do that thing which is least, why take ye thought for the rest? Consider the lilies how they grow: they toil not, they spin not; and yet I say unto you, that Solomon in all his glory was not arrayed like one of these.

If then God so clothe the grass, which is to day in the field, and to morrow is cast into the oven; how much more will he clothe you,

O ye of little faith? And seek not ye what ye shall eat, or what ye shall drink, neither be ye of doubtful mind. For all these things do the nations of the world seek after; and your Father knoweth that ye have need of these things. But rather seek ye first the kingdom of God; and all these things shall be added unto you. Fear not, little flock; for it is your Father's good pleasure to give you the kingdom.

If it is the Father's good pleasure to give the believer all that is necessary to sustain life, I had to ask: Why am I not experiencing the results of this? I submit to you that as the cares of this world made its demands, I lost sight of this truth through inconsistent teaching to which I was exposed. This truth was not consistently put in my path of hearing even though I spent a significant number of hours in church on a weekly basis. This is when I realized that it takes more than hearing one or two messages per week at church to live the abundant life—I had to take responsibility for learning, rehearsing, and applying God's Word to my own life. Taking on this challenge resulted in the lifestyle of faith I share with you in the next chapter. It has been an amazing journey!

END NOTES

[1]Jack W. Hayford, <u>Toward More Glorious Praise: Power Principles for Faith-Filled People</u>, (Nashville: Thomas Nelson Publishers, 1994), 29.

[2]E.M. Bounds, <u>Praying that Receives Answers</u>, (New Kensington: Whitaker House, 1984), 7.

[3]<u>Nelson's Illustrated Bible Dictionary</u>, (Nashville: Thomas Nelson Publishers, 1986), 866-867.

[4]Robert Wise et al., <u>The Church Divided</u>, (South Plainfield: Bridge Publishing, 1986), 131.

[5]<u>Nelson's Illustrated Bible Dictionary</u>, (Nashville: Thomas Nelson Publishers, 1986), 653.

[6]Ibid., 867.

Chapter 3

Faith in Fashion

Faith is the foundation upon which the life of the believer is based, and as one continues to grow in Christ, he must clearly understand what faith is. This is critically important for the believer if he is to enjoy deliverance in every area of life and experience abundant life, for the "just shall live by his faith," (Habakkuk 2:4). So, if the just lives by his faith, he must understand not only what faith is, but the just must know how to appropriate it since "faith, if it hath not works, is dead, being alone," (James 2:17). Scriptures give us definition of faith in Hebrews 11:1: "Now faith is the substance of things hoped for, the evidence of things not seen." To better understand this, this verse could be expressed in the following formula:

FAITH = WHAT IS DESIRED IN THE NATURAL
BUT CURRENTLY EXISTS IN THE SPIRIT.

Faith is not some mystical phenomenon! It is not something that God only gives to apostles, prophets, evangelists, pastors, or teachers. It is multifaceted and is the spiritual fashion statement of the believer. It is still in style. Let's examine this fashion from the following views.

- Faith is that which reaches out into the provisions of God and assures the believer that what he has need of, God has already provided.

- Faith is choosing to wait and trust in the outcome that God said we could have.

- Faith is the proof of things that we cannot see with our natural eyes and enables one to respond to the desired thing as if it were already objects of sight as opposed to things for which one hopes.

- Faith is grace to wait until the fullness of time when the thing desired will be made manifest.

- Faith is the invisible form of something tangible but has not been manifested with substance that the human can interact with his five senses.

- Faith is the process of manifesting the unseen.

That is faith. It is the process in which the unseen takes on a form where mankind can detect and manage the unseen with his senses. Faith is patience to wait for the transition to complete. Once we digest these truths concerning faith, what a difference it will make in our lives. We will increase in our trust in a loving Father whose desire it is to increase us in every area of life.

There is an emotion, which attempts to disguise itself like faith, and that emotion is anxiety. It is imperative that believers do not confuse the element of faith with something that resembles faith. There are many disgruntled believers who have fallen prey to anxiety because they thought being anxious would move the hand of God. The laws that God put in motion, respond to faith, not anxiety or wanting something badly. As believers, we are to "be anxious for nothing but by prayer and supplication let our requests be made known unto God," (Philippians 4:6). We must be confident in knowing that "no good thing will he withhold from them that walk uprightly," (Psalm 84:11b). That is faith in a nutshell—are you willing to "faith it" out until the desired thing comes? Are you willing to "trust it" out in the meantime?

Walking in faith consistently is a learning process. Like the disciples, many ask God to increase their faith. God responds letting us know that we have been given all the faith He plans to give us—He has given us "the measure" of faith. Hence, it is not a faith deficit that is the problem for most; it is a problem in exercising faith through patience. And, in many cases it is doubt, unbelief, and lack of love that block faith from completing its cycle. Faith works by love. How's your love life? Do we approach one another prepared to extend the God-kind of love toward them? Do we extend a love that does not judge? Do we offer a love that accepts one just as one is? Do we extend a love that sees another as God's person? Do we fuel another's life with a love that is blind to the color of his skin? There is more to faith than just naming and claiming a thing. It is indeed yours for the asking, but with the asking there are some required tasks that must be completed. The Bible calls it corresponding action, for faith without works is dead (James 2:17, 20). Holy Spirit will always reveal the action that should correspond to our faith. With that in mind, the statistics of our desired outcome should begin to increase.

The Source of Faith

God has given every believer the measure of faith. "For I say, through the grace given unto me, to every man that is among you, not to think of himself more highly than he ought to think; but to think soberly, accordingly as "God hath dealt to every man the measure of faith," (Romans 12:3). This level of faith is the gateway to salvation. Faith that takes us beyond saving faith comes from One Source, and, that Source is the Word, for "faith comes by hearing and hearing by the word of God," (Romans 8:17). What this passage reveals is that faith is commensurate with the amount of Word that is alive to the believer. Faith does not come from someone laying hands on you or by all the other calisthenics that many practice. Simply listening to messages on tape or at church or by reciting Scriptures is only a part of the means by which faith comes. This is a good start, but there is more to this process than employing the natural mechanics of hearing.

The type of hearing the Bible speaks of is the precise moment in time when Holy Spirit causes us to enter into a knowing or understanding of what we have heard. It is the moment in time when one has to choose to change or deliberately choose to remain the same. It is heart comprehension, not mental comprehension even though our minds participate in the process. It is the divine moment in time in which the Logos becomes Rhema. When understanding emerges, it becomes the foundation upon which one can build his faith. It is indeed important for the believer to consistently sit under sound teaching, but he must also know that having an intellectual response to the Word is very different from responding in the heart. The caution to the believer is that the Word must be a priority, and he must consistently avail himself to the Word, for he cannot foretell the point at which Holy Spirit will cause that Word that he has heard to become Rhema or Truth. This is that which can make you free! This is an appointment one surely would not want to miss.

While each is given the measure of faith, it might appear that some have more than others. This couldn't be further from the truth. The fact of the matter is that some choose to **exercise** their faith more than others, thus it appears that they have more faith.

Types of Faith

Aside from saving faith, there are numerous types of faith. Louis Rushmore describes each type as follows:

TABLE 7

TYPES OF FAITH

TYPE	DESCRIPTION
LITTLE FAITH	"Wherefore, if God so clothe the grass of the field, which to day is, and tomorrow is cast into the oven, shall he not much more clothe you, O ye of little faith," (Matthew 6:30). See also Matthew 8:26; 14:31; 16:8.
GREAT FAITH	"When Jesus heard it, he marveled, and said to them that followed, Verily I say unto you, I have not found so great faith, no, not in Israel," (Matthew 8:10). See also Matthew 15:28.
NO FAITH	"And he said unto them, Why are ye so fearful? How is it that ye have no faith?" (Mark 4:40). See also Mark 6:6.
TAUNTING FAITH	"He saved others; himself he cannot save. If he be the King of Israel, let him now come down from the cross, and we will believe him," (Matthew 27:42).
SAVING FAITH	"And when he saw their faith, he said unto him, man, thy sins are forgiven thee," (Luke 5:20). And he said to the woman, Thy faith hath saved thee; go in peace," (Luke 7:50).
STOLEN FAITH	"Those by the way side are they that hear; then cometh the devil, and taketh away the word out of their hearts, lest they should believe and be saved," (Luke 8:12).

TYPE	DESCRIPTION
LOST FAITH	"And he said unto them, Where is your faith? And they being afraid wondered, saying one to another, What manner of man is this? For he commandeth even the winds and water, and they obey him," (Luke 8:25).
HEALING FAITH	"And he said unto her, Daughter, be of good comfort: thy faith hath made thee whole; go in peace," (Luke 8:48). See also Acts 14:9.
PRECIOUS FAITH	"Simon Peter, a servant and an apostle of Jesus Christ, to them that have obtained like precious faith with us through the righteousness of God and our Saviour Jesus Christ," (2 Peter 1:1).
INCREASING FAITH	"And the apostles said unto the Lord, increase our faith," (Luke 17:5). See also 2 Corinthians 10:15.
FAILING FAITH	"But I have prayed for thee, that thy faith fail not: and when thou art converted, strengthen thy brethren," (Luke 22:32).
HINDERED FAITH	"In whom the god of this world hath blinded the minds of them which believe not, lest the light of the glorious gospel of Christ, who is the image of God, should shine unto them," (2 Corinthians 4:4). See also John 5:44; Acts 13:8.

TYPE	DESCRIPTION
USELESS FAITH	"Nevertheless among the chief rulers also many believed on him; but because of the Pharisees they did not confess him, lest they should be put out of the synagogue," (John 12:42).
FAITH FILLED	"And Stephen, full of faith and power, did great wonders and miracles among the people," (Acts 6:8). See also Acts 6:5; 11:24.
THE FAITH	"Watch ye, stand fast in the faith, quit you like men, be strong," (1 Corinthians 16:13). See also 2 Corinthians 13:5; 1 Timothy 4:1; Jude 3.
OPEN-DOOR FAITH	"And when they were come, and had gathered the church together, they rehearsed all that God had done with them, and how he had opened the door of faith unto the Gentiles," (Acts 14:27).
ERRING FAITH	"Which some professing have erred concerning the faith…," (1 Timothy 6:21).
STEPPING FAITH	"And the father of circumcision to them who are not of the circumcision only, but who also walk in the steps of that faith of our father Abraham, which he had being yet uncircumcised," (Romans 4:12).

TYPE	DESCRIPTION
WALKING FAITH	"For we walk by faith, not by sight," (2 Corinthians 5:7).
LIVING FAITH	"Now the just shall live by faith: but if any man draw back, my soul shall have no pleasure in him," (Hebrews 10:38).
WORD OF FAITH	"But what saith it? The word is nigh thee, even in thy mouth, and in thy heart: that is, the word of faith, which we preach," (Romans 10:8). See also 1 Timothy 4:6.
WEAK FAITH	"Him that is weak in the faith receive ye, but not to doubtful disputations," (Romans 14:1).
VAIN FAITH	"And if Christ be not raised, your faith is vain; ye are yet in your sins," (1 Corinthians 15:17). See also 1 Corinthians 15:2, 17.
HOUSEHOLD FAITH	"As we have therefore opportunity, let us do good unto all men, especially unto them who are of the household of faith," (Galatians 6:10).
JOYOUS FAITH	"And having this confidence, I know that I shall abide and continue with you all for your furtherance and joy of faith," (Philippians 1:25).

TYPE	DESCRIPTION
GROUNDED FAITH	"If ye continue in the faith grounded and settled, and be not moved away from the hope of the gospel, which ye have heard, and which was preached to every creature which is under heaven; whereof I Paul am made a minister," (Colossians 1:23).
STEDFAST FAITH	"For though I be absent in the flesh, yet am I with you in the spirit, joying and beholding your order, and the stedfastness of your faith in Christ," (Colossians 2:5). See also 1 Peter 5:9.
ROOTED FAITH	"Rooted and built up in him, and stablished in the faith, as ye have been taught, abounding therein with thanksgiving," (Colossians 2:7).
WORKING FAITH	"Remembering without ceasing your work of faith, and labour of love, and patience of hope in our Lord Jesus Christ, in the sight of God and our Father," (1 Thessalonians 1:3).
PATIENT FAITH	"Knowing this, that the trying of your faith worketh patience," (James 1:3).
SPREADING FAITH	"For from you sounded out the word of the Lord not only in Macedonia and Achaia, but also in every place your faith to God-ward is spread abroad; so that we need not to speak any thing," (1 Thessalonians 1:8).

TYPE	DESCRIPTION
COMFORTING FAITH	"Therefore, brethren, we were comforted over you in all our affliction and distress by your faith," (1 Thessalonians 3:7).
LACKING FAITH	"Night and day praying exceedingly that we might see your face, and might perfect that which is lacking in your faith," (1 Thessalonians 3:10).
GROWING FAITH	"We are bound to thank God always for you, brethren, as it is meet, because that your faith groweth exceedingly, and the charity of every one of you all toward each other aboundeth," (2 Thessalonians 1:3).
UNFEIGNED FAITH	"When I call to remembrance the unfeigned faith that is in thee, which dwelt first in thy grandmother Lois, and thy mother Eunice; and I am persuaded that in thee also," (2 Timothy 1:5). See also 1 Timothy 1:5.
HOLDING FAITH	"Holding faith, and a good conscience; which some having put away concerning faith have made shipwreck," (1 Timothy 1:19).
FIRST FAITH	"Having damnation, because they have cast off their first faith," (1 Timothy 5:12).

TYPE	DESCRIPTION
FIGHTING FAITH	"Fight the good fight of faith, lay hold on eternal life, whereunto thou art also called, and hast professed a good profession before many witnesses," (1Timothy 6:12).
OVERTHROWN FAITH	"Who concerning the truth have erred, saying that the resurrection is past already; and overthrow the faith of some," (2 Timothy 2:18).
KEPT FAITH	"I have fought a good fight, I have finished my course, I have kept the faith," (2 Timothy 4:7).
COMMON FAITH	"To Titus, mine own son after the common faith: Grace, mercy, and peace, from God the Father and the Lord Jesus Christ our Saviour," (Titus 1:4).
SOUND FAITH	"This witness is true. Wherefore rebuke them sharply, that they may be sound in the faith," (Titus 1:13). See also Titus 2:2.
COMMUNICATING FAITH	"That the communication of thy faith may become effectual by the acknowledging of every good thing which is in you in Christ Jesus," (Philemon 6).
EFFECTIVE FAITH	"That the communication of thy faith may become effectual by the acknowledging of every good thing which is in you in Christ Jesus," (Philemon 6).

TYPE	DESCRIPTION
ASSURING FAITH	"Let us draw near with a true heart in full assurance of faith, having our hearts sprinkled from an evil conscience, and our bodies washed with pure water," (Hebrews 10:22).
PROFESSED FAITH	"Let us hold fast the profession of our faith without wavering; for he is faithful that promised," (Hebrews 10:23).
UNWAVERING FAITH	"But let him ask in faith, nothing wavering. For he that wavereth is like a wave of the sea driven with the wind and tossed," (James 1:6).
UNDERSTANDING FAITH	"Through faith we understand that the worlds were framed by the word of God, so that things which are seen were not made of things which do appear," (Hebrews 11:3).
ACTIVE FAITH	Hebrews 11:4-40.
FOLLOWING FAITH	"Remember them which have the rule over you, have spoken unto you the word of God: whose faith follow, considering the end of their conversation," (Hebrews 13:7).
DEAD FAITH	James 2:14-26.
NOT FAITH ONLY	"Ye see then how that by works a man is justified, and not by faith only." (James 2:24).

TYPE	DESCRIPTION
PRAYING FAITH	"And the prayer of faith shall save the sick, and the Lord shall raise him up; and if he have committed sins, they shall be forgiven him," (James 5:15).
TRIED FAITH	"That the trial of your faith, being much more precious than of gold that perisheth, though it be tried with fire, might be found unto praise and honor and glory at the appearing of Jesus Christ," (1 Peter 1:7).
EXAMINING FAITH	"Beloved, believe not every spirit, but try the spirits whether they are of God: because many false prophets are gone out into the world," (1 John 4:1).
VICTORIOUS FAITH	"For whatsoever is born of God overcometh the world: and this is the victory that overcometh the world, even our faith," (1 John 5:4).
OVERCOMING FAITH	"Who is he that overcometh the world, but he that believeth that Jesus is the Son of God?" (1 John 5:5).
LYING FAITH	"He that believeth on the Son of God hath the witness in himself: he that believeth not God hath made him a liar; because he believeth not the record that God gave of his Son," (1 John 5:10).
TREMBLING FAITH	"Thou believest that there is one God; thou doest well: the devils also believe, and tremble," (James 2:19).

TYPE	DESCRIPTION
HOLY FAITH	"But ye, beloved, building up yourselves on your most holy faith, praying in the Holy Ghost," (Jude 20).

Source: Louis Rushmore, "Types of Faith," Bible InfoNet, 10 September 2001, 1-2.

Faith in God is so paramount to mankind and more so for the believer. It is the lifeline of the believer. It is what the believer lives by. From this list, I would venture to say that those the believer should possess are as follows: little, great, saving, healing, precious, increasing, faith filled, open-door, stepping, walking, living, word of, joyous, grounded, stedfast, rooted, working, patient, comforting, growing, unfeigned, holding, first, fighting, kept, common, sound, communicating, effective, assuring, professed, unwavering, active, following, praying, tried, examining, victorious, overcoming, and holy faith. The types of faith that should be avoided by the believer include: no, stolen, lost, failing, useless, erring, weak, vain, lacking, dead, lying, and trembling faith. Show me a faithless life, and I'll show you a defeated life. Defeat and faithlessness go hand in hand.

Old and New Testament Faith

Though some would argue, the path to salvation in the Old Testament strongly resembles that of the New. Salvation in the Old Testament was primarily built upon faith in God, the Father, while the New was built upon God, the Son. And, since they are One, the same was provided for mankind during both times. The difference is that their expressions were different. Habbakuk 2:4 and Romans 1:17 bear witness in that they both indicate that the just lives by faith. The Apostle Paul indicated that what he taught was already revealed in the Scriptures of old. Using as examples, he referred to David and Abraham as believers of the Old

Testament whose faith justified them. Paul posed a question in Romans 4:1-7:

> What shall we say then that Abraham our father, as pertaining to flesh, hath found? For if Abraham were justified by works, he hath whereof to glory; but not before God. For what saith the scripture? Abraham believed God, and it was counted unto him for righteousness.
>
> Now to him that worketh is the reward not reckoned by grace, but of debt. But to him that worketh not, but believeth on him that justified the ungodly, his faith is counted for righteousness. Even as David also describeth the blessedness of the man, unto whom God imputeth righteousness without works, saying, Blessed are they whose iniquities are forgiven, and whose sins are covered.

Hebrews 11:3 points to creation and reveals that it was faith that caused the worlds to be formed by the word of God and that it was faith that caused the unseen to be seen. And, so it is, faith in the Old Testament is the faith that was transmitted throughout the New. The expression of faith in the New is different in that Holy Spirit now dwells in the believer as opposed to resting upon an individual as in the case of the Old. So, the magnitude of the work that He is able to do is magnified tremendously. It is by faith that believers today can say, "Let there be," and things that do not exist come into being. This is so because believers have right-now access to the throne of God as a result of the magnitude and New Testament expression of Holy Spirit. This expansion in His assignment allows Him to do works in greater proportion. I had to learn to be thankful for the far excellent way that has been extended, for the covenant that Jesus now mediates is "a more excellent ministry, by how much also he is the mediator of a better covenant, which was established upon better promises," (Hebrews 8:6).

The Presence of Faith in Today's World

The faith that started in the Old Testament and traveled on throughout the New was and is further transmitted to the believer today. It leaves a trail of experience among believers that support the notion that faith is critical in the life of the believer. If the believer is going to be successful in this day as times grow more wicked and wiser, this will occur only if he "lives by his faith," (Habbakuk 2:4). To those who perpetuate the name-it-and claim-it philosophy and seek microwave results through prayer, you must consider the element of faith. To function in this level of faith requires a full persuasion in God and full persuasion that He will do just what He has said He would do. The problem with believers is that many do not spend the time necessary to hear from God. As a result, they pray amiss, or they ask in violation of the plan that God has designed for his life, "for this is the confidence we have in him, that if we ask any thing according to his will, he heareth us: And, if we know that he hears us, whatsoever we ask, we know that we have the petitions that we desired of him," (1 John 5:15-16). Many "ask and receive not, because, ye ask amiss, that ye may consume it upon your lusts," (James 4:3). From this, the believer can conclude that he can have whatsoever he desires as long as the thing desired is the will of God and not the desire of fleshly lusts.

What You Say Is What You Get

One of the most deadly weapons to the success of the believer is a simple vice. That vice is the tongue. Many are defeated because the things they say do not align with what God says about them. In fact, this is something that begins early in life for so many. For example, some mothers, out of anger with their mates, tell their sons that they are just like their no-good daddy, and men make such derogatory sayings to their children regarding their mothers. From this, children learn to speak derogatory remarks to each other and extend it to their peers and playmates. And, as they have been told, that is what they grow up and become except through divine intervention. James 3:10 put it this way: "Out of the same mouth proceedeth blessing and cursing. My brethren, these things ought not to be." As I pondered this passage in my heart, I was moved to consider the functions of the mouth using this analogy. It is with the mouth we dine on succulent foods. But, in some instances, the body refuses to process the food ingested. As a result, regurgitation comes up and flows out of the mouth. So, at one point something good flows through the mouth, and later regurgitation (something bad) flows through the mouth. This is not a pleasant analogy, but it makes a very strong point. When the body is functioning properly, this will not happen. James is saying that we should not allow blessing and cursing to flow through the same mouth as believers. We should be far more stable in our ways.

In the words of Charles Capps, "God's Word that is conceived in your heart, then formed by the tongue, and spoken out of your own mouth, becomes a spiritual force releasing the ability of God within you,"[1] The flip side of this is that satan will do everything within His power to cause the believer to speak the total opposite of what God has spoken.

Those that say they can and those that say they can't are both right. Words are the most powerful thing in the universe. The words you speak will either put you over or hold you in bondage. Today, many Christian people have been taken captive by their own words.[2]

Because many have practiced so long saying the wrong thing, it will take practicing to unlearn such behaviors. Some will say it doesn't take all of that. But, I am persuaded that believers must make deliberate attempt to alter their speech. The believers who desire to be successful must commit to making this character adjustment and must be consistent in the practices that it will take to unlearn such behaviors. Believers must hear what God says through His leaders and Holy Spirit. They must see what He is saying through the reading of the Word. And, they must say what God has said. These three gateways help to establish a strong foundation upon which the believer can stand on the promises of God and experience the richness of His blessings.

Subject to Change

Salvation includes many aspects of deliverance. First and foremost is the opportunity to accept a gift that grants all who will receive forgiveness of sin. By making this step, the gateway to many other benefits is opened. "While we look not at the things which are seen, but at the things which are not seen: for the things which are seen are temporal; but the things which are not seen are eternal," (2 Corinthians 4:8). This means that one of the associated benefits is that when the enemy preys upon the believer, the believer can have hope because any physical or naturally observable thing that the enemy has imposed, is subject. What power is it subject to? It is subject to change. That condition does not have to remain. This is most powerful! That which is affected in the physical through the senses can be replaced by what it becomes subject to in the spirit. For sickness, we can have health. For poverty, we can have provision. For unrest, we can have peace. It is this hope and applying biblical principle to situations that will aid in causing the believer to live in such abundance.

As one who was reared in a faith-filled household, I am so thankful because of the legacy my parents left me. That legacy consists of lessons based on faith and demonstration of that same faith. As a result, I continue to grow into a woman of faith due in part to the life they lived before me. The faith I have today is the faith I received through hearing the Word of God. How to appropriate my faith is something I caught from them as they did not compromise and partner with doubt and unbelief. They never gave up in spite of what came against them. They fought a good fight; they kept the faith; and, they finished their course.

END NOTES

[1]Capps, Charles, <u>The Tongue: A Creative Force</u>, (Tulsa: Harrison House, 1964), 7.

[2]Ibid., 8.

Chapter 4

My Secret Is Out

Praise and worship is a subject of combined potency and one that I had checked off as mastered on that inherited checklist I told you about earlier. This universal mandate from God is given to everything that has the capacity to breathe. It is so much more than what meets the eye. I had to learn this because if I did not feel anything, I did not bring forth praise. And, in some instances, I was embarrassed to express my true self openly—I was too cool for that. This excuse worked for me until one day I was asked, "When you are in need of My help, guidance, or intervention or even before you express your need for My help and the answer you need is provided, do I tell you, "I am too cool for that?" That was the day I offered up a true sacrifice of praise and worshipped in spirit and truth. And, I didn't care about what I looked like, what I sounded like, or what others thought about me. That is the day when my private praise became a public experience. My secret was out!

Praise relates more to all that God has done while worship gives tribute to who God is.

If worship is an umbrella, praise is the center pole that we hold. Praise is a meaningful facet in the process and event of worship. Praise is a verbal act.[1]

For all that God has done for me, praise and worship are not mere options. They are mandatory because all breathing beings silence the rocks by giving God praise. Failure to do so will result in the rocks' crying out (Luke 19:40) in our place. Whether this is to be interpreted literally or symbolically, that would be a shame. Psalms 150:6 declares, "Let everything that hath breath praise the Lord. Praise ye the Lord." Such like commands can be found throughout the Scriptures, particularly in the Psalms. What is implied in this verse by virtue of the command are two occasions when God is to be praised: when we feel like it and when we don't.

> Praise has many facets, as does the very character of God. There are seasons for expressing joy and seasons for morning—times in which we celebrate triumph and times when we praise Him in the valley, by faith, for His ability to work a miracle. There are times when we feel like praising God and times when we invoke the will and regardless of our emotional state, we praise Him simply because He is worthy.[2]

Praise is one of the central elements to the believers' faith in Christ, and we must be reminded that praise is a command and not a choice. This is not Burger King—no one is going to hold the pickles or onions and put it all on a sesame seed bun as you place your order. One thing I am learning about our Father is that when He says something, He means it. But, when He repeats Himself, He really means it! We must praise!

The Presence of Praise in the Old Testament

Praise has its origin as far back as the beginning of time when God Himself spoke of the work of the Trinity declaring that what "He had made . . . it was very good," (Genesis 1:31). Long before God made man and created the earth, as man knows it, He created an angel in the third heaven whose sole purpose was for playing and orchestration of music. This angel, Lucifer, was so uniquely designed that musical instruments were built into his body. Lucifer was one among the three angels who were most highly ranked. Michael was the archangel for war and protection of God's people. Gabriel was the angel of God's presence who announced and interpreted God's plans for the future; and, Lucifer was the priestly angel of music, praise, and worship of God.

This plan of praise and worship remained intact until the point when Lucifer decided that he wanted to be like God. When he was cast down from heaven and stripped of the name, which meant *morning star* as a result of the revolt he lead in glory, I believe that is the point at which mankind was given the ability to praise—that which was stripped from Lucifer. I believe this is why satan, once Lucifer, tries to distract the believer from praising God. All the more important it is for the believer to offer the sacrifice of praise when at times it might hurt or seem to pose an imposition.

An example of this occurred when Miriam sang a song of victory that led the Israelites to a successful crossing of the Red Sea. To us, this might not have been a good time to be dancing and singing a song. But, it is apparent that Miriam understood how God uses simple things that might not make sense to carnal minds and sad to say, it might not have made sense to some who believe.

> Miriam the prophetess, the sister of Aaron, took a timbrel in her hand; and all the women went out after her with timbrels and with dances. And Miriam answered them, Sing ye to the Lord, for he hath triumphed gloriously; the horse and his rider hath he thrown in to the sea (Exodus 15:20-21).

The presence of praise in the Old Testament continued its journey throughout the times and found a special residing place in David, the youngest son of Jesse and later king of Israel. The book of Psalms, which is a collection of prayers, poems, and hymns that focuses on the praiser's thoughts of God in praise, captures David's expression and offering of praise unto God. The word *psalm,* simply put, is a song that is to be sung to the accompaniment of some type of musical instrument. Psalms were used in both public and private worship. David was one who had no issue with either. In fact, the Scriptures reveal that he "danced before the Lord with all his might," (2 Samuel 6:14). That means he held nothing back. He did not allow people to define him and dictate how he should express himself to his God. This is the message that has to be communicated today. Praise may or may not be something you feel like doing, and that is fine because praise is not contingent upon how one feels. It is the result of obedience. And, that is what is key. Are we willing to obey as God has commanded?

The Presence of Praise in the New Testament

While there is a very strong presence of praise in the Old Testament, it is equally as strong if not stronger in the New Testament. It remained an integral part in the life of the believer. For every instance God moved on behalf of the people, the spontaneous reaction was praise. In John 9:24 reference is made to a blind man that was healed, and the people proclaimed, "Give God the praise . . . ."

Paul gives an account of the impact of praise in one of his imprisonments:

And at midnight Paul and Silas prayed, and sang praises unto God: and the prisoners heard them. And suddenly there was a great earthquake, so that the foundations of the prison were shaken and immediately all the doors were loosed. And the keeper of the prison awaking out of his sleep, and seeing the prison doors open, he drew out his sword, and would have killed himself, supposing that the prisoners had been fled. But Paul cried with a loud voice, saying, Do thyself no harm: for we are all here. Then he called for a light, and sprang in, and came trembling, and felt down before Paul and Silas. And brought them out, and said, Sirs, what must

I do to be saved? And they said, Believe on the Lord Jesus Christ, and thou shalt be saved, and thy house (Acts 16:25-31).

This passage is so powerful! It illustrates how praise can be a gateway to salvation and can deliver one who is captive by setting them free. It also illustrates that praise pricks the hearts of those who do not believe. Something must be wrong when we offer up sacrifice to God, and there is no reaction from God returned. This moves me to pose a question: Where is the potency in our praise? It appears that yes many are screaming and shouting hallelujah, but there are no results that follow.

A similar result is evidenced in Acts 3:2-10:

And a certain man lame from his mother's womb was carried, whom they laid daily at the gate of the temple which is called Beautiful, to ask alms of them that entered into the temple; Who seeing Peter and John about to go into the temple asked an alms. And Peter, fastening his eyes upon him with John, said, Look on us. And he gave heed unto them, expecting to receive something of them. Then Peter said, Silver and gold have I none; but such as I have give I thee: In the name of Jesus Christ of Nazareth rise up and walk. And he took him by the right hand, and lifted him up: and immediately his feet and ankle bones received strength. And he leaping up stood, and walked, and entered with them into the temple, walking, and leaping, and praising God. And all the people saw him walking and praising God: And they knew that it was he which sat for alms at the Beautiful gate of the temple: and they were filled with wonder and amazement at which had happened unto him.

In this passage we see praise as a gateway to witnessing. Since this tool worked so effectively, believers today can use it as an example to create opportunity to share the good news.

One final passage on this subject is found in Acts 2:44-47 where the saints went from house to house praising God for the great things He had done. The end result was that "the Lord added daily to the church such as should be saved," (Acts 2:47). From this passage, I base my assumption concerning the strong presence of praise in the New Testament. I believe that in their going from house to house praising God, they encountered people that were not necessarily saved in all of those households, and not all of those encountered in passing were saved. If they all were saved, then the passage would not have included that many were saved daily. I believe that what strongly impacted the unsaved was the strong presence of praise to God by the believers. And, since God inhabits the praises of His people (Psalm 22:3), there was a very strong presence of God on the scene as they went from house to house. That is what made the difference. This is the message that has to be perpetuated throughout Christendom.

The Sacrifice of Praise

The only acceptable form of sacrifice as revealed in the New Testament is the sacrifice of praise. While mustering up the want-to to offer up praise, all must resolve that any living being that can breathe is commanded to praise the Lord. And those who partake of Jesus' righteousness are to "rejoice in the Lord, O ye righteous: for praise is comely for the upright," (Psalm 33:1). We are to "offer the sacrifice of praise to God continually, that is, the fruit of our lips giving thanks to his Name. But to do good and to communicate forget not: for with such sacrifices God is well pleased," (Hebrews 13:14-15). Do you want to please God? Then praise Him! Praise is what all who breathe air are to do. Doing things God's way always leads to a power that flows only through obedience. When we are obedient to the command to praise, there is a power that comes with each expression of praise.

There is a power in praise that invokes Holy Spirit.

And Elisha said, As the Lord of hosts liveth, before whom I stand, surely, were it not that I regard the presence of Jehoshaphat the king of Judah, I would not look toward thee, nor see thee. But now bring me a minstrel. And it came to pass, when the minstrel played, that the hand of the Lord came upon him (2 Kings 3:14-15).

There is a power in prayer through which prophesying comes through instruments:

Moreover David and the captains of the host separated to the service of the sons of Asaph, and of Heman, and of Jeduthun, who should prophesy with harps, with psalteries, and with cymbals: and the number of the workmen according to their service was: Of the sons of Asaph; Zaccur, and Joseph, and Nethaniah, and Asarelah, the sons of Asaph under the hands of Asaph, which prophesied according to the order of the king. Of Jeduthun: the sons of Jesuthun; Gedaliah, and Zeri, and Hjeshaiah, Hashabiah, and Mattithiah, six, under the hands of their father Jeduthun, who prophesied with a harp, to give thanks and to praise the Lord (1 Chronicles 25:1-3).

There is a power in praise that drives evil spirits away.

And it came to pass, when the evil spirit from God was upon Saul, that David took an harp, and played with his hand: so Saul was refreshed, and was well, and the evil spirit departed from him (1 Samuel 16:23).

From this information alone, one should be convinced that any sacrifice given to praise God is well worth the sacrifice. I am so glad I learned to clap my hands and shout unto God with a voice of triumph and thanksgiving in my heart in spite of how I feel or what condition I am in physically, mentally, emotionally, financially, or spiritually. He gets the praise.

Worship: The Higher Dimension of Praise

Just in case you did not know, the Father is looking for you and me. And, when we praise, He makes his invited entry to the scene. He himself declares that He lives on the inside of the praises of His people. Now, I know why my mom and dad made music throughout the day every day. Mom sang and would clap her hands as she walked throughout the house. Dad would sing or whistle, pull out his harmonica, or play the guitar after a long hard day of work. They were inviting God to show up in the midst of whatever situation was at hand whether good or bad. I can truly say that He always showed up and manifested Himself in some tangible way.

Earlier we established that the prelude to worship is praise. On the other hand, worship is the higher dimension of praise. The term worship comes from the Hebrew word "shaba," which means to "bow down" or to "prostrate one's self." Though most commonly referred to as a noun, the essence of what worship is primarily consists of action. Praise is extended to God for what He does. Worship is praise and reference to God for who He is. Over time it becomes clearer that our appreciation will not allow us to wait for God to do something dramatic before we spend time with Him through praise and worship.

Worship is the graduated state of praise that is a privilege extended to those who are in a position to worship God in spirit and truth.

> For the hour cometh, and now is, when the true worshippers shall worship the Father in spirit and in truth: for the Father seeketh such to worship him. God is a spirit: and they that worship him must worship him in spirit and in truth (John 4:23-24).

When one considers the tenets of worship, the bountiful blessings of God, acknowledgement of His awesome wonder, the epitome of holiness, His mercy and grace, and the reality of His love, one would have to deliberately quench the spirit to avoid entering that special place of intimacy with God. As the believer enters into that special place by moving from the space of praise to the zone of worship, it is at this point that he is able to behold the glory of God. It is the point at which God is consumed and breathes in through His nostrils the fragrance of His righteousness that He has put upon the believer. This experience is commensurate with the believer's knowledge of the Word.

> The more you know God through His Word, the more potent your prayer and worship is. You cannot pray or worship above your knowledge of God.[3]

Worship is what believers do. It is a lifestyle. And, because it is an act of the will in the spirit, it is something that can be done without anyone even knowing what is going on especially if one is in a place where it is inappropriate to shout out "Halleluja," for instance, the workplace. And, the good thing about this is that God set it up such that He does not give specific procedures to follow in how one chooses to worship except when He instructed believers to do so in spirit and in truth. New Testament instructions for praise and worship give unrestricted liberty to the worshipper allowing for creative expression to the Father. Thus, worship can take on any form.

> As preachers, we worship as we declare the Word of God to our congregations. As corporate worshippers sitting in the pew, we worship as we listen to the Word of God. As individuals, we worship when we feed on the Word of God and apply it to daily living.[4]

For those who deliver sermons, those sermons become sacrifices of worship.

> Preaching becomes a sacrifice of praise when it exalts the Person of truth . . . preaching engages people in worship when it explains and expounds the gospel of Jesus Christ. When the gospel is explained, God's people are edified, the unsaved are evangelized, and the truth of the Word pierces the soul and spirit (Hebrews

4:12). A man of God can preach without worshipping—and the Word will not return void. But a man of God truly experiencing the joy of worshiping in spirit and in truth will never preach the gospel without worshiping.[5]

So, whether you are one who only sits in the pew or one who ministers to those sitting in the pew, God expects praise—He expects worship.

"Cause" Worship

Becoming a life-long worshipper is the goal for the believer. As I held numerous discussions with individuals regarding their walk in Christ, the one thing that was common among most is that they had been taught that in order to praise and worship God, they must first feel something. This is an untruth that has to be brought down. God never commanded people to praise and worship as a response to what they feel. We praise, and we worship because it is what we have been commanded to do.

Life-long worshipers are determined, zealous to follow Christ regardless of circumstances. They have grown to prioritize Christ in their life until, as Editor Kent R. Wilson has observed, 'Worship is not just a service I attend. It is a life itself lived out before God.'[6]

What Happens When You Leave Your Water Pot at the Well?

Examples of the new way of worship occur several times in the New Testament. One instance occurred at Jacob's well where Jesus revealed that the way worship once was would no longer be. See the following account.

When therefore the Lord knew how the Pharisees had heard that Jesus made and baptized more disciples than John. Though Jesus himself baptized not, but his disciples. He left Judaea, and departed again into Galilee. And he must needs to go through Samaria.

Then cometh he to a city of Samaria, which is called Sychar, near to the parcel of ground that Jacob gave to his son Joseph.

Now Jacob's well was there. Jesus therefore, being wearied with his journey, sat thus on the well: and it was about the sixth hour. There cometh a woman of Samaria to draw water: Jesus saith unto her, Give me to drink. For his disciples were gone away unto the city to buy meat. Then saith the woman of Samaria unto him. How is it that thou, being a Jew, askest drink of me, which am a woman of Samaria? For the Jews have no dealings with the Samaritans.

Jesus answered and said unto her, If thou knewest the gift of God, and who it is that thou wouldest have asked of him, and he would have given thee living water. The woman saith unto him, Sir, thou hast nothing to draw with, and the well is deep: from whence then hast thou that living water? Art thou greater that our father Jacob, which gave us the well, and drank thereof himself, and his children, and his cattle? Jesus answered and said unto her, Whosoever drinketh of this water shall thirst again: But Whosoever drinketh of the water that I shall give him shall never thirst; but the water that I shall give him shall be in him a well of water springing up into everlasting life. The woman saith unto him, Sir, give me this water, that I thirst not, neither come hither to draw. Jesus saith unto her, Go, call thy husband, and come hither. The woman answered and said, I have no husband. Jesus said unto her, Thou hast well said, I have no husband: For thou hast had five husbands; and he whom thou now hast is not thy husband: in that saidst thou truly. The woman saith unto him, Sir, I perceive that thou art a prophet. Our fathers worshipped in this mountain; and ye say, that in Jerusalem is the place where men ought to worship.

Jesus saith unto her, woman, believe me, the hour cometh, when ye shall neither in this mountain, nor yet at Jerusalem, worship the Father. Ye worship ye know not what: we know what we worship: for salvation is of the Jews. But the hour cometh, and now is, when the true worshippers shall worship the Father in spirit and in truth: for the Father seeketh such to worship him. God is a Spirit: and they that worship him must worship him in spirit and in truth (John 4:1-24).

In this demonstration of the new advent of worship in spirit, there are several key points that must be noted. With every act of obedience, there is some type of inevitable benefit linked to the obedience. Worship is so critical because not only does it invite God to come on the scene, it releases His hand to move.

Let's examine this passage more closely. First of all, Jesus defies tradition by engaging a Samaritan woman in conversation knowing how the Jews looked down on the Samaritans. Samaritans were Jews but were viewed as unpure Jews. This gesture coupled with what Jesus was about to make her aware of, lets me know that freedom in the spirit crosses all religious, ethnic and racial backgrounds. Jesus chats with the woman for some time, and before it was all over, she came to grip with some issues in her life. She was so excited that she took off running and left her pot at the well. She forgot all about her natural need and ran to proclaim Jesus' worth to others in the city because He had met her spiritual need. The pot was a valuable commodity in those days! When it was empty, the emptiness was the indicator that a need had to be met—someone had to fill that pot with water again. The thing that I find amazing with this passage is that she left her pot (which represents her need) at the well where Jesus was. What a place to leave your need! She casted her care upon Him because He openly and truly demonstrated that He cared for her (1 Peter 5:7). When we enter into worship, one thing that should happen is that our need should become insignificant as we minister to the God we love and serve. Significant life-changing events take place when one leaves his water pot at the well and goes on to be about our Father's business.

As we grow in knowledge concerning spiritual things, we must understand that "the weapons of our warfare are not carnal, but mighty through God to the pulling down of strongholds . . . ," (2 Corinthians 10:4). What are strongholds? A stronghold is anything that repeatedly succeeds in influencing you to do the opposite of what God has commanded you to do. The good news is that we have been equipped with what we need to overcome people, powers, and principalities that try to do this. Our weaponry consists of an arsenal of the Word, prayer, praise and worship. There's that combination again: praise and worship. Remember, this is the combination that brings God to any scene where help is needed. We know this because "God inhabits the praises of His people," (Psalms 22:3). He takes up residence in our praise.

With this combination of weaponry, the Word of God, direct access to God through prayer, praise and worship, how much more do we need? Here's what I discovered. We do not need more; we need to make consistent use of what we already have because Who we have working in us is far greater than what comes against us. It is time for the believer to rise up and purpose in his heart to do things God's way. His way of doing things does not require man's approval. Doing things His way and employing these tools are what brought the Old Testament followers through great trials and tribulation. It is what brought the New Testament believers through. The requirement is no different for believers today. Because satan's previous assignment was to worship God, and because he was stripped of such a privilege, his worst enemy is the believer. Believers have a song that the angels cannot sing, not even satan. That song is <u>Redeemed, My Soul Has Been Redeemed</u>. If we want to put the enemy at bay, it is imperative that we offer up sacrifice of praise and worship to God in spirit and in truth. It is time for "the redeemed of the Lord to say so," (Psalms 107:2a). It is time to put this great power into action.

Change: The Acid Test for Worship

Worship is central to our faith in Christ. The implications for the true discipline are all encompassing, for worship is more than an event on Sunday morning—it becomes a life-style. True worship will spill over into the week—informing choices, determining perspectives, offering a cup of cold water, loving the unlovely, practicing fidelity, and a cluster of other wholesome actions and attitudes. These attributes may, in fact run counter to our culture. For the Christian who pursues the worship of a holy God will pursue a holy life-style as a natural by-product."[7]

In the passage regarding the Samaritan woman, it is pretty obvious that she had sought fulfillment of a spiritual thirst through natural things even though she could clearly articulate what her religious ritual consisted of, a ritual that brought her no sustaining fulfillment. We also observed how when the Samaritan woman accepted the fulfilling and life-giving water that Jesus would give and entered into true worship, the end result was that her life was changed. No matter how much one dances and shouts, the true sign of worship is that one will change. There should be some signs that one has had an encounter with God as in the case of Isaiah. When Isaiah had a one-to-one consultative confrontation with God, he walked out of that encounter with a changed life. His preaching changed. The words that flowed from his mouth changed. He was a totally new creature. That is the same impact worship is to have today. It is not about stroking God's ego, that is, if He has one. It is for us to create an atmosphere where we can stand in His presence under true light, see how holy He is and how far we miss the mark, and implore His help to make us whole. In this we see that worship is for man more so than it is for God.

END NOTES

[1] Jack W. Hayford, <u>Toward More Glorious Praise: Power Principles for Faith-Filled People</u>, (Nashville: Thomas Nelson Publishers, 1994), 82.

[2] Ibid., 85.

[3] Dr. Tony Evans, "The Concept of Worship" on the Urban Alternative, WMBI in Chicago.

[4] Vernon M. Whaley, <u>The Dynamics of Corporate Worship</u>, (Grand Rapids: Baker Books, 2001), 148.

[5] Ibid., 149.

[6] Jack W. Hayford, <u>Toward More Glorious Praise: Power Principles for Faith-filled People</u>, (Nashville: Thomas Nelson Publishers, 1994), 146.

[7] Ibid., 35.

Chapter 5

A Glimpse of Real Living

Because I did not know the simple truths I have shared with you, I was almost destroyed. It is a sad state of affairs not to know, but it is worst not knowing that you do not know. There was a season where I was emotionally unstable. My finances did not meet my basic needs. My spiritual life was defunct and was not attracting others to desire this thing Christians call salvation, and the list goes on. In a nutshell, I was not living up to my maximum spiritual potential in a day when "He gave some apostles, some prophets, some evangelists, some pastors and teachers for the perfecting of the saints," (Ephesians 6:10). Scripture supports this claim in that it states, "My people are destroyed for a lack of knowledge," (Hosea 4:6). When the Word of God is not received with God's expressed intent for what that Word should accomplish in the life of the believer, misaligned expectations are developed. When this happens, the disillusioned one holds God accountable for things to which He never said or committed. I did that.

If having abundant life in Christ is the goal for Christians, it begins with gaining knowledge of what the whole walk entails. The progression of growing in grace includes receiving consistent teaching of the Word of God, getting an understanding of the Word, and finally applying the Word through faith. When the believer applies the Word that he already knows on a consistent basis to every area of life, that is the level of abundance he will experience, for we prosper naturally in proportion to spiritual growth (3 John 2). There is no workaround. The key to warring against spiritual retardation and even spiritual death is to become spiritually adept in the Word of God through undergoing systematic and continuous teaching of the Word, and by applying the Word daily in every area of life. That is what real living looks like.

For years ministers have preached to the people the "what to do," but seldom did they adequately give definition of the "whats", nor did they clearly define how to do that which was required of believers. Although churches have grown in this area, others have a long way to go. If Christians are going to be successful by God's definition, all must get an understanding. Understanding comes by consistently sitting under sound delivery of the Word whether the teaching comes directly by illumination of Holy Spirit or whether it comes via the teaching of a spiritual leader.

While it is the plan of the Lord to redeem, it is satan's plan to keep the Body in a state of not knowing. The adversary knows that knowledge is power. He also knows that applying knowledge is more powerful. If he can keep us from knowing, he will never have to worry because we will not have anything to apply. His goal is 2 for 1—keep them from knowing, and keep them from applying.

As I feel the palpitations of the heartbeat of God, I hear His concern about knowledge as He Himself declares, "My people are destroyed for the lack of knowledge," (Hosea 4:6). The rejection of knowledge can be subtle as well as blatant. Subtle rejection of knowledge occurs when we do not make time for it. In my observation of life, we create space in our lives to accommodate those things we really want to do. While we rely on the leaders in the church to teach us, we must add to this through "study and show ourselves approved unto God a workman that needeth not to be ashamed rightly dividing the word of truth," (2 Timothy 3:16).

Although it is an old cliché, the same can be said regarding the spiritual things—"ignorance is not bliss." What you do not know from a world perspective can cost you your job, house, car, or natural life. What you do not know from a spiritual perspective can cost you abundant living in time as we know it, and it can cost you your eternal life, which is simply knowing Jesus in our now and beyond the dispensation of what we call time.

My goal was to share with you some simple truths that I did not know. And, when I was not getting the results that I thought I should have been getting, I confronted God respectfully. I said to Him: "Either you are real or you are not. Show me!" That is when I heard an inward voice speak to me saying, "I have been waiting for you right here. Now, I can help you because you have sincerely invited me in." My life has never been the same.

So, what does real living look like? Some will lead you to believe that real living is reflected in fashionable cars, elaborate homes, who you know, where you work, what you wear, etc. My profile of real living is quite simple and has nothing to do with things and their associated values. My assessment of real living is based on that which cannot be perceived through man's five senses. Real living is as follows:

1. Working at fostering your relationship with God
2. Consistently increasing in the Word of God through diligent study and prayer
3. Giving unconditional praise
4. Rendering sincere worship
5. Discipline and relationship with God attracting others and causing them to desire what brings you this kind of joy
6. Peace in the midst of apparent storms
7. A steadfast stand that in spite of what I see, think, or feel, God is who He says He is
8. Properly aligned expectations of God and others

This is the profile of real living.

I close by saying, "It is my prayer that some word or phrase will provoke you to becoming rooted in what God has said to us through His Word. I pray that you, 'receive with meekness the engrafted Word which is able to save your souls,' (James 1:21). I pray that you will 'grow in grace and in the knowledge of our Lord and Saviour Jesus Christ,' (2 Peter 3:18) so that you can have life and that more abundantly,' (John 10:10). Look and live!"

BIBLIOGRAPHY

Anders, Max E. 30 Days to Understanding the Bible. Dallas: Word Publishing, 1988.

Authur, Kay. How to Study the Bible. Eugene: Harvest House Publishers, 1994.

Bertolini, Dewey M. Back to the Heart of Youth Work. Wheaton: Victor Books, 1989.

Bevere, John. Breaking Intimidation. Lake Mary: Creation House, 1982.

Bisset, Tom. Why Christian Kids Leave the Faith.: Grand Rapids: Discovery House Publisher, 1992.

Bounds, E.M. Praying that Receives Answers. New Kensington: Whitaker House, 1984.

Capps, Charles. The Tongue: A Creative Force. Tulsa: Harrison House, Inc., 1976.

Chrnalogar, Mary Alice. Twisted Scriptures. Grand Rapids: Zondervan Publishing House, 2000.

Conner, Kevin J. The Church in the New Testament. Portland: City Bible Publishing, 1982.

_____. Interpreting the Scriptures. Portland: City Bible Publishing, 1983.

Copeland, Germaine. A Call to Prayer. Tulsa: Harrison House, Inc., 1991.

Cornwall, Judson. Let Us Abide. South Plainfield: Bridge Publishing, 1977.

Crawford, Dan R. DiscipleShape: Twelve Weeks to Spiritual Fitness. Peabody: Hendrickson Publishers, 1998.

Dake, Finis Jennings. Dake's Annotated Reference Bible. Lawrenceville: Dake Bible Sales, Inc, 1989.

DePree, Max. Leadership Is An Art. New York: Dell Publishing, 1989.

Dunlop, Cheryl. Follow Me As I Follow Christ: A Guide for Teaching Children in a Church Setting. Chicago: Moody Press, 2000.

Evans, Tony. Guiding Your Fmily in a Misguided World. Wheaton: Tyndale House Publishers, 1991.

_____. The Carnal Christian. Dallas: The Urban Alternative, 1993.

_____. Today's Alternative: Enter His Presence Daily. Dallas: The Urban Alternative, 2000.

Garlington, Joseph L. Worship: The Pattern of Things in Heaven. Tulsa: Destiny Image Publishers, Inc., 1998.

Gehris, Paul D. and Katherine A. The Teaching Church Active in Mission. Valley Forge: Judson Press, 1987.

George, Bob. Classic Christianity: Life's Too Short to Miss the Real Thing. Eugene: Harvest House Publishers, 1989.

Gills, James P., M.D. The Dynamics of Worship.: Tarpon Springs: Love Press, 1992.

Hunter, Frances. <u>Possessing the Mind of Christ</u>. Kingwood: Hunter Books City of Lights, 1984.

Hagin, Jr. Kenneth. <u>Speak to Your Mountain</u>. Tulsa: Rhema Bible Church, 1993.

Hagin, Kenneth E. <u>Casting Your Care Upon the Lord</u>. Tulsa: Rhema Bible Church, 1993.

_____. <u>Exceedingly Growing Faith</u>. Tulsa: Rhema Bible Church, 1988.

_____. <u>How to Turn Your Faith Loose</u>. Tulsa: Rhema Bible Church, 1998.

_____. <u>The Believers' Authority</u>. Tulsa: Rhema Bible Church, 1990.

_____. <u>ZOE: The God-Kind of Life</u>. Tulsa: Rhema Bible Church, 1997.

_____. <u>The Real Faith</u>. Tulsa: Rhema Bible Church, 1989.

_____. <u>What Faith Is</u>. Tulsa: Rhema Bible Church, 1989.

Hayford, Jack W. <u>Toward More Glorious Praise: Power Principles for Faith-Filled People</u>. Nashville: Thomas Nelson Publishers, 1994.

Jacobs, Cindy. <u>Possessing the Gates of the Enemy</u>. Tarrytown: Chosen Books Publishing Company, LTD.:, 1991.

Kinnaman, Gary. <u>Dumb Things Smart Christians </u>Believe. Ann Arbor: Servant Publications, 1999.

Martin, George. <u>Reading Scriptures as the Word of God</u>. Ann Arbor: Servant Publications, 1998.

Maxwell, John C. <u>Developing Leaders Around You</u>. _____: InJoy, Inc., 1995.

_____. The 21 Indispensable Qualities of a Leader. Nashville: Thomas Nelson Publishers: Nashville, 1999.

Mears, Henrietta C. What the Bible Is All About. Ventura: Regal Books, 1963.

Nee, Watchman. Christ The Sum of All Scriptural Things. New York: Christian Fellowship Publishers, Inc., 1973.

Nelson's Illustrated Bible Dictionary. Nashville: Thomas Nelson Publishers, 1986.

Richards, Lawrence O. Christian Education: Seeking to Become Like Jesus. Grand Rapids: Zondervan Publishing House, 1975.

Robertson, Palmer O. The Christ of the Covenants. Phillipsburg: Presbyterian and Reformal Publishing Company, 1980.

Rushmore, Louis. "Types of Faith". Houston: Bible InfoNet, 2001.

Scroggie, W. Graham. How to Pray. Grand Rapids: Kregel Publications, 1985.

Tkach, Joseph. Transformed by Truth. Sisters: Multnomah Publishers, Inc., 1997.

Torrey, R.A. How to Study the Bible. New Kensington: Whitaker House, 1985.

_____. What the Bible Teaches. Peabody: Hendrickson Publishers:, 1998.

Trent, John Ph.D., Osborne, Rick, Bruner, Kent. Parent's /Guide to the Spiritual Growth of Children. Wheaton: Tyndale House Publishers, 2000.

Turabian, Kate L. A Manual for Writers. Chicago: University of Chicago Press:, 1987.

Warren, Rick. Dynamic Bible Study. Wheaton: Victor Books, 1981.

Whaley, Vernon M. The Dynamics of Corporate Worship. Grand Rapids: Baker Books, 2001.

Wiersbe, Warren. Bible Commentary: New Testament. Nashville: Thomas Nelson Publishers, 1991.

_____. Bible Commentary: Old Testament. Nashville: Thomas Nelson Publishers, 1991.

Wigglesworth, Smith. Dare to Believe. Ann Arbor: Servant Publications, 1997.

Wilhoit, Jim. Christian Education and the Search for Meaning. Grand Rapids: Baker Book House, 1998.

Wilkinson, Bruce H. Dr. The Prayer of Jabez: Breaking Through the Blessed Life. Sisters: Multnoman Publishers, 2000.

Wilmington, H. L. Dr. Wilmington's Guide to the Bible. Wheaton: Tyndale House Publishers, Inc, 1984.

Wise, Robert et al. The Church Divided. South Plainfield: Bridge Publishing, 1986.

Word Ministries, Inc. Prayers that Avail Much. Tulsa: Harrison House, Inc., Tulsa, 1980.